Praise for *Into the World Outspread*

"Renato Rosaldo's poetry catapulted me into navigating the world with a disability. My gratitude for doing so with a scientist's accuracy, a bodhisattva's compassion, and a poet's grace."

— **Sandra Cisneros**

"Renato Rosaldo is one of those rare poets who speaks in many different registers and to diverse readerships. *The Day of Shelly's Death* combines poetry with anthropology in a breathtaking volume. *The Chasers* transforms testimonies from the author's high school Mexican American gang into moving prosody. Now Rosaldo gives us *Into the World Outspread: Notes from a Walker*. The last word in this title can be read as someone who walks the earth and writes eloquently of the experience, as well as a mobilization device for the physically impaired. If you doubt this is poetic material, you would be wrong. Rosaldo continues to stun us with his insight, feeling and grace. A compelling book!"

— **Margaret Randall**, author of *Stormclouds Like Unkept Promises*

"I don't know how he does it. Renato Rosaldo writes about the hardest subjects with grace, accuracy, and love. His tender apprehension of details, images and scenes soars above the struggles, as his poems offer greater understanding of poetry's presence in all of life's moments. What a powerful voice!"

— **Naomi Shihab Nye**, Young People's Poet Laureate, Poetry Foundation

"When we enter Renato Rosaldo's *Into the World Outspread: Notes From a Walker*, we are never waylaid because each poem in this down-to-earth collection connects at the heart of human matters great and small. Walking becomes an act of mediation, mindfulness, and a ritual of healing."

— **Yusef Komunyakaa**, Pulitzer Prize-winning poet and author of *Everyday Mojo Songs of Earth*

"*Into the World Outspread: Notes from a Walker* brings Renato Rosaldo's growing body of poetry before readers who have found in his earlier volumes a poet who explores social and cultural identity, parenting, personal tragedy (the still-unexplained death of his first wife), and a life of the mind. In this lively, frank, and sometimes discomforting collection, his poems consider aging, illness, injury, and recovery. Here the 'experts' are many, but only a few know what is wrong, and the poet is fortunate in his openness to listen to them all and find what helps him to recover. These are poems that shake their fist at suffering while thanking family, friends, and a trusty walker for a body compromised, but a life fully lived."

— **Patricia Spears Jones**, author of *A Lucent Fire: New and Selected Poems*

"Collapse, falling, buckling, derramado—your body spilled across the floors of daily life. It is not the daily life you once had before the stroke. It is not the same body you once inhabited. Your questions are radical now—the future, the transitions, recovery, the new 'Exotic dance of pain,' your placements of 'leg, pelvis and torso' are central to your new life. This book does not buckle or wince or fear. Rosaldo does not pull back. His poems are fearless. His 'notes' are precise, studied, balanced on ripped tendons. The stranger with a new face in the mirror faces the 'out of place' body. The poems become his 'walker.' Centimeter by centimeter, the speaker drags, collapses, hopes and floats in between worlds toward the luminous 'inner jaguar.' This collection is astounding in its bodies of structure, line, pace and layers of story, remembrance, hope—and its meditations and maps of suffering and transcendence. This is a poetry for this exact moment—Enlightenment, healing rising, pinnacle of Rosaldo's writing career."

— **Juan Felipe Herrera**, United States Poet Laureate
Emeritus

Into the World Outspread

Other poetry by Renato Rosaldo

The Chasers
The Day of Shelly's Death
Diego Luna's Insider Tips
Prayer to Spider Woman/Rezo a la mujer araña

Into the World Outspread

NOTES from a WALKER

Renato Rosaldo

Casa Urraca Press

A B I Q U I Ú

Cover illustration by Bill Florez.
Author photograph by Barbara Byers.
Set in Le Monde Livre Std, Swear Display, and Mr. Rafkin.

25 24 23   2 3 4 5 6 7

First edition

ISBN 978-1-956375-08-4

CASA URRACA PRESS

an imprint of Casa Urraca, Ltd.
PO Box 1119
Abiquiú, New Mexico 87510
casaurracapress.com

To my grandchildren, Gabo, Micah,
Ari, Antonio, and Edan.

Your relations have sustained and inspired me.

Contents

Part Three: Notes from a Walker

I

II

III

Into the World Outspread

PART ONE

Notes from a Walker

September 1996

I.

I'm chair of Anthropology.
The dean has been meeting behind my back
with the sociobiologists, all white men.

I'm a Chicano.
The cultural faculty are six people of color
    (two men, four women),
three white women, and a white man.

The sociobiologists insist the conflict
is between science and non-science (alias nonsense).
They never mention white maleness of their science.

My meeting with the provost changes nothing.
I suggest the sociobiologists form their own department.
They refuse.

Mary asks me not to teach this fall.
I meet the students and say class is cancelled.
My speech slurs. (Do they think I'm drunk?)
burden intolerable   being chair   war zone
    must cancel   cannot do it   so sorry

My head is ringing as I walk across quad.
Claudio from Chile wants to talk.
My right leg is energized, left foot drags.

I'm speaking Spanish with Claudio,
aim key at lock in office door.
It falls, clacks to floor, and I fall.
Claudio shouts, *Algo terrible está pasándote.*

The department secretary dials 9-1-1,
Claudio races to find Mary.
An ambulance speeds me to Emergency.

II.

After a few days in intensive care I'm sent home
with pills, an immediate change of pace,
meetings abruptly halt, full stop.

I lie in bed, utterly still, exhausted
by stroke, days pass

until in my mind's eye, I see a line of poetry,
written longhand, fine penmanship, purple ink.

I try to shoo the verses away,
never wanted to write poems,
but they insist.

I surrender,
copy the verses down,
do a painting with each poem,

call them healing songs,
find a teacher, Judith Bishop.
I did not choose.

After My Stroke

Today my walk stirs
an old joke about the spastic
in an auditorium. To loud applause

he glides an ice cream cone
toward his mouth, but the crowd gasps
as it smashes into his eye.

I contort on my toes,
then lurch on a flat floor.
My lips abruptly pinch

into a crooked smile,
more symptom than self-expression.
I know. This time on me.

Claudio Durán

A Chilean Ph.D. student at Stanford, Claudio was released
from Villa Grimaldi, an interrogation and torture center
    under Pinochet.
While there, he stumbled over the body of a friend,

mangled, barely conscious on the ground after torture.
Claudio glimpsed him underfoot and bent over to help.
The butt of a long gun convinced him to move on.

I was talking Spanish with Claudio when I collapsed
on the floor by my office door. Next time he saw me,
Claudio spoke English, asked if I still spoke Spanish.

He said, *Un amigo mío perdió el español después de su embolia.*
Dijo que lo mismo me podría haber pasado.
No quería avergonzarme al hablarme en español.

Claudio dijo que yo no tenía idea, pero quería que yo supiera.
Cuando me vio derramado sobre el suelo, pensó, esto es como
Villa Grimaldi, pero esta vez podré ayudar a mi amigo.

Fear of Collapse

Long ago, my then-wife stumbled,
dropped over a ledge
into a swollen river below,

loss left me afraid of falling,
being mired in bottomless muck.

To fend off terminal descent
I pretend to skim over the surface,

wear down my shoes more on the outer
than the inner edges.

Years later a stroke.
My right leg buckles,
pelvis grabs and swings,

then torso saves from collapse
and throws weight
back on other leg.

My Right Leg Wobbles

No feeling

in leg

over my ankle.

No stability

support from earth, gone

none I can count on.

Paralysis is

more absence than presence

hard to detect.

In the mirror

my face gives

no sign of comprehension.

Season of fear

time of obscurity

without visible end.

Black Flip-Flops

At the corner store I buy
a pair of thick-soled black flip-flops
built to last longer than the flimsy thin
rubber ones I usually buy.
I indent the black ones
into the shape of my soles,
increasing my attachment to them.
They slowly wear into a signature
of the jagged character I call my gait,
how I'm recognized, perhaps who I am.

From the Floor

I turn on the furnace, finish breakfast,
and drop down dizzy, following
my blood pressure to the floor.

Mary phones the nurse who drones, *Call 9-1-1.*
From beneath a blanket on the floor
I listen to sirens, louder and louder,
then silence, then footsteps thumping.

Fire engine, ambulance, five paramedics
burst in, give oxygen, record blood pressure,
plop me on gurney.

I am an Emergency, plugged in,
monitored until late afternoon when
the doctor declares, *It was nothing,
you can go home now.*

An Academic Good-Bye

In three weeks I'll move
to the other coast. After thirty-three
years I'll celebrate my departure.

This gathering is an antidote
to mornings spent sorting through
hanging folders filled with letters,
my accumulated past.

Nobody mentions terror
in manila folders,
where dittoed pasts rage
through purple smudge.

Last words from friends teeter
along tender edges of sincerity laced
with sarcasm. If remembered, I'll be missed.

From a Shovel

Don't give me trouble
give me a shovel.

I was a victim and hungry when I had possessions.
　　I'm a shooting star woman, they say.
The wolf beam woman leaps at my throat.
　　I'm a woman who shouts, they say.
I beat my wings against dreams.
　　I'm a woman of light, they say.
Gray vipers ride a plump baby
　　and strike at the baby's throat, they say.
Jesus our woman,
　　I'm a woman who whistles, they say.
Water full of flowers　　our infant admiral,
　　I'm a woman tossed up out of the earth, they say.
a white corpse of light　　infinitely sobbing.
　　I'm a completed woman-man, life-giver, life-taker, they say.

　　　　Restfully babbling　　pushing perfect grass
　　　　toward the explosion of coming dawn.

Out of Place

This man might be St. Francis.
He wears a tan-and-white hooded robe,
clasps his hands, a gourd above his shoulders,
a squirrel peeks from behind that gourd.
He's on his knees, in prayer
or contemplation of the yet unborn.
He stands against a dark backdrop,
his profile illuminated by the moon
over a New Mexico highway
with only his nose and chin visible
as if he wants not to be known.

He meditates about imponderables,
what is yet to come, how his body will age,
its infirmities, how it will disappoint,
the laughter of his nephews and nieces,
how he will endure letting go of those most dear,
how he will stay the course of his meditation,
the ripples of pain ascending his back,
his wonder at kneeling on Route 66
finding he's out of place.

Limping Along

At my age it's hard to keep from looking ahead,
wondering what it'll like to be older than my seventy-three.
Who will I be? I peruse my elders, in their nineties,
feeble and forgetful, but their sense of humor intact.

Bob and Nancy live next door. Bob drives his Buick
up our lawn, almost into our living room.
Nancy won't have far to walk. She wobbles
five steps as Bob's arm supports.

They've come for a drink, his rum and Coke,
her Fresca. Nancy asks, *What was I
about to say?* Bob tries to tip her off,
chuckles, *What were we talking about?*

Don Luis Leal

He carried an epoch on his back,
obras, nombres, fechas,
their weight precisely recalled.

With him a generation, gone.
Like an Aztec emperor-to-be, he walked
the longest time, the largest stone on his back.

Even at one hundred, after he'd outlasted the others,
he kept walking the burden,
his chuckles lightening the load.

I remember his canas, already in 1956
at the Hotel Del Parque in Guadalajara
where my brothers and I rode

the elevator incessantly, made
him climb the stairs. Even yesterday
his look still scolded, then his eyes sparked

and he said, *Te conozco, ladrón de elevadores.*
Le dije, *Te conozco, eras cuate de mi papá,*
¿Qué haces tú, aquí en estos tiempos?

Luego nos abrazamos, nos reímos.
Ahora nos despedimos, prendo
una velita morada. Pobre de nosotros.

My Birthday

My grandson Gabo says,
Baba, you're seventy-four now,
that's why your walk.

He replicates my limp
with uncanny precision,
step/dip/lurch to the right.

Next day I walk downstairs
to the R train at 28th.
A homeless man waves his arms,

Let him through,
one day you too will be old.

At McDonald's a woman asks
how I'm feeling, gives me
her place in bathroom line,

pats my shoulder,
I always help cripples.

In Brooklyn on my way to the subway
at Flatbush and Fulton,
over my shoulder, I spot

three pre-teen boys dip and lurch,
copycats. *Cool pimp walk.*

A man shimmies
in my path,
Keep up that swag!

Last Days

I.

I hate knowing my mind is going, says Nana Dot,
my sons' grandma. Reassurance doesn't help.

We invite her to spend the weekend.
I meet her bus, but she's not on board.
The driver says, *An elderly lady got off at the last stop.*

I race to Madison and 32nd. Too late. She's gone.
I call 911 and a squad car drives me around. No luck.

The cops take me home, say, *Try to remain calm.*
Rest assured, they say, *She'll turn up.*
This is New York City, not the jungle.

II.

My mother falls again, smacks her head on the floor.
My brother phones, *Come home. Mom makes no sense.*

At the hospice I sit next to her, her hair done for my visit.
This is a wedding chapel, see the bride and groom over there?
Two patients hold hands.

Mom says, *That man's a cop. He thinks I'm a princess.*
The employee treats her well.

My arm cradles her. She leans into my shoulder,
closes her eyes, her breath gentle.

Not certain she can hear me, I read her Emily Dickinson.
Perhaps you'd like to buy a flower? But I could never sell.

She squeezes my hand,
recites the rest, eyes still closed.
A week later, on Good Friday, *Death kindly stopped for her.*

Granada

Long ago Louise blessed our newborn love
with hers, at parties her eyes sparked blue,
she always sang, once danced on the table.

Next month she'll be ninety-seven, a year since I've seen her.
She's changed, won't know who you are, her son says.

Slumped in a chair, unable to hear,
unable to see, she seems absent. I give her a hug,
a kiss, hold her parchment hand and shout in her ear.

She nods her head and I burble into laughter.
Granada—she says, never could say Renato—
you haven't changed a bit.

PART TWO

Daño / Injury

September 2003

At my New York book launch my body feels alien.
Muscles I try to move do not respond.
I arrived today from Saltillo, northern Mexico,
where my poetry collection was published.
I moved two weeks ago from Palo Alto to Manhattan.
My body now feels as unfamiliar as the city.

When I walk Biscuit the sidewalk tilts,
drops me to the ground, but in an hour I feel better.
My son Manuel takes me to yoga.
As we walk home, I feel new energy in left leg,
let my right foot drag. I lie, tell Manuel I'm fine.

Back home, unpacking boxes overwhelms,
books and more books.
I'm caught   between   searching
     for bookcases   and ordering   built-ins
from   the Greeks   down the street.

I see the doctor I first met last week.
His exam, *Show me your smile,*
touch your fingertips, one by one, faster,
says, *You've suffered a stroke,* asks me to walk
three blocks to Emergency, the fastest way there.

I call Manuel, sob as I tell him I've had a stroke.
He says, *Cry, let it all out.*

My Fall

I'm in Oakland, October 9, 2016,
Mary strides into health food store.
I strain to keep up, step street to sidewalk,
abruptly drop, slam knee into concrete.
I hear a voice, *Help. Help me,*
crumple, cannot breathe,
will not let my leg be touched.
A thin young black man draws near,
offers to carry me in his arms.
Mary tells him, *No, you'll hurt yourself.*
He then delicately lifts limp body,
slides it into car, brushes my knee on front seat.
I howl louder and louder.
He tries again, leaves my knee untouched.
I sob in gratitude, hold his hand.
Why I fell remains obscure,
gravity wilding.

Crawling Along

Mary and I land in Oakland for the birth
of Ari, our third grandson, after Gabo and Micah.

Repetition does not lessen my delight at again becoming
a grandfather. What I find diminished with age is my ability
to be awake the entire night and function the day after.

Our daughter, Olivia, is stolen
by her night of labor. The morning after, I hobble to kitchen,
cling to the wall in search of Cheerios.

My fall was the day before.
I lean along the kitchen counter until my shoulders flop
as the floor yanks me backwards.

I can't breathe, call for help. Crawl toward living room,
where my son-in-law, Noam, says he's got me.

We drive to a nearby storefront clinic.
Noam insists I use a wheelchair to get in door.

Pain throbs like last night's moon as they lift me to gurney.
They X-ray my knee, tell me it's not broken.

I cannot climb the twenty-one steps to visit Ari at home.

My Right Knee

In Oakland I see an acupuncturist
who embodies healing, his persona crafted for the job,
his father, his father's father, back six generations,
practiced the family trade in China.

He binds poultices to my knee, warm and moist,
pungent odor of Chinese herbs, my knee turns black,
yet pain lessens. He believes in poultices but
ruptured quad tendon is not in his vocabulary.

Walking is precarious for me
on his driveway's downward slope.
I borrow a battered walker, navigate the slope in fear.

Don't hurry, don't fall again, he says.

Almost a Year

I'm at a writers group
in Owen Sound, Ontario,
but after our two-hour workshop
I can't get up from my chair.
Danuta, the convener, says, *You're really weak.*
I'm left feeling mortified,
mumble about atrophied quad muscles.
With knowing touch, she gets me up from my chair,
tells me to see Jason, a physiotherapist she helped train.
He has a studio in Wiarton,
a town of twelve hundred at the foot of Georgian Bay
near our cottage in Red Bay.

He feels my knee and asks,
Do you know your quad tendon is ruptured?
I say, *Not only do I not know,*
but I have no idea of what that is.
He says, *Your quad tendon attaches*
kneecap to quad muscles.

He tells me to see an orthopedic surgeon
who will order an MRI and confirm his diagnosis.
Surgery must be done right away.
Jason says, *It's been almost a year since your injury,*
almost too late to do your surgery.

I hold my breath and wobble along
between too late and the nick of time.

I Ask My Doctor

I want your advice,
whether to do surgery
on my ruptured quad tendon,
at least that's what Jason, the Canadian
physical therapist, says it is.
It's been almost a year since my fall.

Tell me what you'd say
to your father if he were in my shoes.
You know summers in Canada, I walk and kayak.
You tell me, *The surgery is for you,*
not for couch sitters, like my dad,
worth the agony of long recovery.

As I step out the door, you say,
Remember the surgery could fail,
but it's your only chance.

Three Physical Therapists

Physical therapists use an individual's history and physical examination to arrive at a diagnosis and establish a treatment plan.

—Wikipedia, "Physical therapy"

I.

In Albuquerque, a month after my fall, the physical therapist says, *The quad muscles in your right leg have atrophied.* But says nothing about why they deteriorated or what I should do to recover. I work and work, exercises to strengthen my quads. I sit, lift my right foot until leg straightens, tighten my quads, over and over, again and again. I trudge behind my walker. The walker is insurance against another fall. I cannot fall again. My quads fail to strengthen. I ask why they fail. The physical therapist does not respond.

II.

In Brooklyn, back home, three months later, I choose a nearby physical therapist who is attached to a dance studio. He echoes the physical therapist in Albuquerque, says *Your quad muscles have atrophied.* But insists that the deterioration is due to my stroke of 2003, not to my fall of 2016. Why would he say this? I insist that the fall was what damaged my body. He says, *I'm the expert, you're the patient.* He says, *You have so much strength in your right leg, you can't have a ruptured quad tendon.* Over a year later, when I've removed the leg brace and recovered from surgery, I tell him the actual diagnosis of my injury is I had a ruptured quad tendon. I thought he would like to learn about the diagnosis, confirmed by MRI and the surgery. He insists his reasons for thinking as he did were, and still are, sound. Perhaps he can't hear. Maybe he fears a lawsuit. Perhaps he's simply an arrogant son of a bitch who refuses to learn from his mistakes.

III.

When I'm back in New York City, I see James, a physical therapist who has a studio in Manhattan. He checks my knee, confirms Jason's diagnosis. He advises me to get an MRI and consult three orthopedic surgeons. If two or all three agree to do the surgery, I should pick one and go ahead. If only one says yes, he tells me to forget about the surgery. All three in fact say they can do it. I pick one. James has me practice sitting to standing and other transitions I'll need while recovering from surgery. He tells me to keep doing my exercises. I'll need all the strength I can muster in recovery which will be arduous. It won't be over when the surgery ends. I must hope, must hope it works, best chance to heal from my injury.

In the Recovery Room

In Manhattan, October 3, 2017,
Mary walks me to surgery.
A white-coated attendant escorts me through operating room.
He assures me as we glide past menacing machines,
then a resident hooks me to IV.
Next stop, he says, recovery room.

He tells me to see *Krippendorf's Tribe*,
the film about an anthropologist who searches
but fails to find a lost tribe.
To salvage reputation, he invents the tribe,
has family members play savages, films
them to document his discovery. No more words.
All abruptly goes black.

I cannot decipher recovery room,
cannot parse marble walls, high ceilings,
a room of scant recuperation.
Odor of alcohol permeates, neon lights glare.

I don't know where I've been, what happened,
where I'm going, is it over or yet to come.
As if an apparition, Mary glides by.

The surgeon walks up, raises right hand,
crosses his fingers, his version of prayer.

He looks in my eyes, stops mid-word, says
he'll explain to Mary, briskly walks away.

Mary returns, says surgeon said he could not use
cadaver graft as planned, delicately tugged tendon down thigh
until it reached full stretch, all the while fearing it would snap,
a complication, massive apprehension,
time consuming, labor intensive,
at last attached tendon to kneecap.

I want to leave.
Nurse says she'll stay,
slides me onto gurney,
wheels me to room for the night.

Behind a black curtain,
my roommate sobs, tells nurse
his pain, on a scale of one to ten, is a ten.
I have no pain, but know
his tears won't let me sleep the night.

Dawn.
The resident arrives, pale, slender, sandy hair.
I remember *Krippendorf's Tribe*,
say I remember him.
He pronounces my sentence:
twelve weeks in a brace, right leg locked straight,
day and night, in bed, on toilet,
standing from sitting.
I gasp.

The Procession

In the hospital I awaken.
Our son Sam sits beside me, heart open.
My heart unfurls.
In low tones I talk,
tell what I remember of surgery,
the invented tribe,
a recovery room,
the surgeon's crossed fingers.
Mary arrives, open heart, a red rose.
Health aid enters,
then physical therapist,
last to arrive the occupational therapist.
She locks my right leg straight in a brace.
Surgeon said leaving hospital is not a problem.
I sign release forms.
I ride wheelchair from my room to elevator,
then to taxi waiting at ground level below.
The driver, a man from Puebla, pulls me
tenderly across back seat.
We speak Spanish. Mi corazón se desdobla.
The health aid cradles my right leg.
Sam and Mary stay at my side.
At home we replay
the entrance in reverse,
right leg out first.
I teeter on left leg.
Sam lifts me.
I plop into transporter chair,
am wheeled in building,
am backed into elevator,
ride it up to our home.

Before Momentum

Nurse insists, *Five milligrams, Percodan.*
Physical therapist will make you move,
then you'll be in pain. You must stop pain
before it gains momentum.

I'm Percodan constipated, but in no pain.
At home, right leg brace straight,
I plop on elevated toilet seat
Mary bought for the recovery period,
wobble back up,
slide peg-leg forward,
push left leg down,
an exotic dance.

I've taken Milk of Magnesia,
gone back to bed.
Turds drop in towel on bed,
humiliation perhaps better than constipation,
for me,
but not for Mary.

Am in no physical pain,
have been in none,
feel as vulnerable as the sky.

Ode to My Tendon

You hold together
muscle and bone,
quad and kneecap.
I nurture you,
sit you in sunsets,
show you
butterflies in flight.
Blades of grass brush us.
I inhale your aroma,
seek your pliable strength
through furtive glances,
behind a tree of lilacs in bloom.
You grow stronger, more elastic,
attach firmly to my kneecap,
support the bend of my leg.
You link bone and muscle.
You grow more pliable,
you grow more powerful.
Sunsets, butterflies,
lilacs in bloom,
blades of grass.

Jaguar

Jane, a healer with knowing, gentle, touch, has often given
me balance and breath. She exhorts,
Listen to the tissues of your quad tendon,
hear their cells, empathize,
your fall severed them, left them amputated,
left them utterly undiagnosed for almost a year.
Bathe them in your tears, caress them,
nourish them with collagen, eat lots of jello.

The tissues of your quad tendon have stretched taut.
They must act like brakes as you descend the slightest slope.
Your tendon left its post, curled up your thigh,
forced other tissues to work unfamiliar jobs.

As your tendon labors, whisper, massage it.
Its cells have become blank. Let them transform.
Tell them to color—red, blue, yellow, green.
Allow them to dance, harmonize and coordinate.

Call your inner jaguar.
Let it ripple through your right leg,
where it marinates,
locked straight in a brace.

I talk with the cells in my tendon,
I ask them to heal.
I ask them to strengthen.
I ask them to dance.
I ask them to breathe.
I ask my inner jaguar to ripple and stretch.

Cough

A month after surgery, good friends,
university teachers, age-mates, all of us gray,
laugh through a fine meal Mary made,
huachinango a la veracruzana.

I think of having to stand from sitting,
stretch my right leg under raised table,
sit on a high hard cushion. Our first dinner party
in the month since surgery.

Next day, I wake up, throat scratchy,
curse whoever passed this on to me.
Cough through the night, spend next two days in bed.
A month after surgery.

I pile up pillows, lie on my back,
leg locked in the brace,
I'm used to sleeping on my belly.
At last, I drop off, spend another day in bed,
still coughing, but less and less.
A month after surgery.

To My Tendon Cells

I beg for your support.
Please be supple and strong,
be easy to bend, hard to break.
I'm to blame,
my fall severed you,
I'll try with my every fiber
not to slam down again,
not to amputate you again.
Please heal now,
harmonize,
sway in sync,
expand and contract in rhythm.
Let me give you
all that nurtures.
I seek collagen, in jello,
to enhance your elasticity.
Your strength is pliability,
more like water than rock,
the grace and power of flow.

Toilet Dance

My right leg is locked straight
in a brace, lightweight metal and Velcro.
I slide my leg forward as I sit down,
aim for a smooth landing,
try not to plop on seat,
must calibrate my descent.
Now I push up with my arms,
drop weight in left leg as I stand,
struggle to keep my balance.
This is as hard as it sounds,
but I've grown more adept.
I've learned a new dance.

January 22

I see my surgeon who says,
*Keep your right leg locked
straight in the brace.*
It's not easy to walk,

transfers are a challenge,
getting on/off toilet,
in/out of bed,
in/out of a chair.

In bed, on my back,
I can't roll over.
Even when we're
next to each other,
Mary, I can't embrace you.

I imagine my surgeon has
not gotten on/off
toilet with a peg leg,
in/out of a chair.

My healing will require time,
right leg locked brace-straight.

My leg will grow weak from immobility,
will mend and strengthen
through physical therapy.

Slender and Supple

My quad muscles had atrophied so much,
the surgeon could not attach a cadaver tendon,
as he planned, to repair my ruptured quad tendon.

Instead he attached my aged tendon, knee to muscles.
It came home to familiar soil.
I try to detect the renewed presence of my aged tendon.

I seek signs, but find none,
no ripple, no bulge, no new stability.
It is back in the place it knows most intimately,
the place where it may become flexible.

One day it will support
my weight and bend,
not break,
no more than a blade of grass.

Slow Fall

On my morning walk
I go farther than I've gone before.
My personal best.
I go to Flatbush past McDonald's.

As we return
I fatigue
and tell Karen, my Trinidadian health aide,
I'm fine.
She nods.

As I near home
I see David on a bench out front,
sitting the pleasure of his morning cigar.
I go toward him, say hello.
My walker catches a brick.

I fall.

I fall forward
as if in slow motion, go limp
as I've been taught to do,
let my body down easy.

I can't get up.
David asks if I need help.
I say I do.
He and Karen lift me up.

I feel no pain.
This is not a repeat of my injury.
Today I am fortunate.

Though it seemed slow to me,
Karen says my fall was so fast
she couldn't catch me.

Knee Bend

The surgeon hoped to attach a cadaver tendon
from my kneecap to my quad muscles,
but they were so atrophied he could not.
Instead, he attached my own tendon to my kneecap,
feared my aged tendon would be so brittle
it would leave my knee with no bend.

Now he tests my knee bend, declares
fifty degrees of bend. I weep with joy,
finding it effortless to bend my knee.
The surgeon adjusts leg brace, says
when seated I can bend knee.

He says that when I walk, sleep, stand from chair,
get on and off the toilet, I must keep leg straight.
I still weep tears certain I'll get the bend I need.

No Wonder You're Called a Walker, Mi Andador

You are a traveler. You go where I go.
You are my constant companion. You walk where I walk.
No wonder you're called a walker.

You step over the curb when I do, so glad you're light in weight.
Other people tell me you should have a seat so I can stop
        and rest.
They don't know you need to be light so I can lift you
        over the curb.

You are just right for me as you are, don't change a thing.
The physical therapist urges me to walk with you
so I can go farther, faster, not suffer another fall.

A black plastic leather container in front
where two pairs of parallel bars come together,
V-shaped, sleek streamlined look.

A three-wheeler, three big wheels,
metal tubes, black with blue splash.
Little boys envy me because of you.

PART THREE

Notes from a Walker

I

Mama Emilia's House

I fondly remember
Mama Emilia's house, squared round a patio.
My uncle says it's a guest house,

but at four I didn't know what that is.
Mom reminds me cousin Irma shattered
my clay pots, transformed me into a fury.

I can still see her cackle
as I jump up and down, icicle daggers
penetrating my skull.

The daggers recalled excavate
memories of the lumpy bed
where mustiness contorts my nose as I stare

at red crepe paper covering the window
to shield eyes fevered with measles.
In the dark of night I walk

cold, uneven, tiles, stand and retch,
then sit with diarrhea. Next morning,
chamomile tea, toast, no butter.

In a Mexican Market

I walk by stalls,
shades of vegetables,
yellow, green, red displayed
in delicately arranged piles.

I sit on a pale green bench
the table covered
with oilcloth, floral designs
blue plastic plates.

I order apple soda
and a quesadilla served
in shredded cabbage
dripping with crema.

Childhood admonitions
possess me. *You'll get
amoebas from eating
food in the market.*

Mary discerns discomfort
teases that I'll suffer
diarrhea in the afternoon,
death by dawn.

The Sheriff and the Bandido

Pancho Villa robs a bank in Columbus, New Mexico,
rides into stereotype, is branded a *bandido*.
The sheriff, of course, swaggers in from his suburban rancho,
a white flight zone outside Waco.
Dressed in ironed jeans and a prep-school smirk, he swears,
I'll slam that desperado in the hoosegow,
forty-eight hours to surrender.
Once again, as you've guessed, Villa slips into the hills,
eludes General Pershing whose horse prances on tiptoes,
leads a military caravan that trails Villa by miles.

In a Mexican Town

The cop leans on a stone wall,
watches me park, smiles my way

as my bumper noses the red line.
We exchange glances, he nods,

I wave and stroll to the plaza
for a slow lunch. I walk

back to the car, find
a yellow ticket nestled under

the windshield wiper.
Our nodding relationship betrayed,

I scribble a long mental note—
the check's in the mail—and chuckle.

After a long drive to the house,
I see the cop took my license plate.

Must drive back to that town, pay the fine,
Friends say I have no choice.

Perfecto Flores

Back in Fowler, where it all began,
Perfecto caresses a naked woman's moist contours,
allows a scorpion, a niño de tierra,
to witness their union blessed by breaking day.
Let my lust for Leonora be undiminished, he prays.

He drives a dilapidated Chevy Caprice,
labor camp to labor camp, grapes shriveling in the sun,
shadows of birds bobbing on waves of heat.
Let me walk the valley of the shadow.
Beauty and grace by my side, he prays.

He carries a red toolbox for the chance odd job.
The other men call a job well done a Perfecto Flores.
He barters know-how for the loyalty of Estrella,
thirteen years old, claw hammer and crescent wrench,
tools for literacy, v like the split of a hammerhead.

At dusk he walks from the fields,
puffs of dust drag behind him,
row after row, sun upon sun.
He stands unblinking, refuses to be short-changed.
May the boss drown in a vat of molten cash, he says.

Lo Prohibido

ICE states its mission: *to protect national security,*
enforce immigration laws, fight crimes and terrorist activity.

In Manhattan, the phone woke me.
My daughter, Olivia, called from Oakland,
told what José, her fourth-grade student,
told her that morning. Face flushed, eyes wide,
he spoke only Spanish, el idioma
en que pudo decir lo prohibido.
On his way home from César Chávez Elementary School
in Richmond, the migra called ICE asked,
Who in your house has no papers?
I'm a citizen, born here, the boy said.
As José arrived home,
the migra burst in,
dogs straining on leashes.
The boy's eyes fixed
on jaws, snarls, white teeth.
His family has papers,
but, in five days, José will be sent
back to Mexico, where he's never
walked home from school.

Vicissitudes of Idioma

*In bilingual settings outsiders and newcomers are often
mystified by the subtle signs and understandings that
determine the language chosen.*

    —Anonymous sociolinguist

In Brooklyn, on my way, I stop at Pedro's taquería, seeking
    a wisp of comfort.

Tables on the sidewalk,

        inside, dark as a cave, Puerto Rican plena, tacos,
            beers, barstools.

Yellow paper circles blossom on the walls and announce,

        beef tacos, on the left   on the right, veggie tacos

           margaritas and tamales in between

bargain prices everywhere

a list nowhere   no menu to be seen.

A woman heats tortillas, fills them with beans, rice,
    and guacamole.

I ask where she's from. She's from my dad's hometown,
    Minatitlán, Veracruz. I exhale.

I sit to eat. Another woman, thin and pale, tends bar. Same
    as me, she eats a veggie taco,

        the absence of beer.

I order a Pacífico, pronounced en idioma, but she misses her cue,

speaks only English to me.

I'm tongueless in a blind alley, surge of fear, until I dare

say, *Buen provecho,* y luego platicamos un buen rato
    en español. She's Puerto Rican,

another etiquette about initiating idioma.

Downhill the East River, and I walk almost there.

II

Into the World Outspread

Both eyes in utter darkness on all sides

Fire to the bottomless force of outward luster

The terror of joy   swallowed up in mind   with head uplifted

The burning dark   heaven in hell   astonishes

The sun's great burning wheels

hollow the flood

A temple rips

against the spiked fence

Ezekiel sees

his eyes wander   the moment dazzling arms appear   behind the moons

an ascending pile   sound the tempest bees   from the ground

We dance

to the smallest   forms of silence   beyond imagination

from distant   celestial descent   strange fire

not our   proper motion   without hope of end

At
our heels
blackest light
plunges us
into flames
each rock
changed now
by words
eyes sing
unobserved tempest
beneath height

Return to Rio

Possessed by an excess of imagination,
Roberto returns to Rio, unable to bear
the thought of being buried in South Bend.

In his mind, a mechanical winch lowers casket,
his cadaver will freeze and thaw.
In Rio, he and I walk a street lined with palms,

gnarl of aged roots, vines glisten their slither.
On Ipanema Beach a young man kisses
his lover
delicately
stroking her bare ass.

I close my eyes, hear only vendors, one chants,
another sings his wares, a barefoot man sambas,
beneath his green umbrella a row of bikinis jiggles.

Ink and Color on Silk

The deer nests behind a black rock.
The Manchurian crane settles on the other side.
Each hooks its neck and looks
at the other—an instant captured.

Between them, the rock looms,
and a plum tree, white flowers
blossom with shades of pink.
Uphill, a pine bough shivers.

The deer with antlers,
the crane with scarlet crown.

A Corner of Her Veil

In ancient times a saintly Sufi man dreamed
    he worshipped a false idol in Greece.
He went to Greece and saw a Christian woman
    on her balcony.
Resplendent as the full moon, she pondered
    the things of her god.

To bask in her radiance, the morning star loitered
    above her bedroom.
To glory in the shining of her black hair, the noonday sun
    darkened for a spell.
In response to the beauty of her dimples, the laughing earth
    folded into an indentation.

The woman's brows were tender sickles over twin moons,
    her lashes a thousand daggers.
The sight of her ruby lips made an old lizard pucker,
    her eyes lured a thousand lovers.
She lifted a corner of her veil and ignited
    the saintly man's heart.

Her hair coiled around his hips and he began to undulate
    like an enchanted cobra.
A single strand of her hair touched his loins, and he forgot
    the name of his god.
His faith was strewn by the wayside like a thousand
    unstrung beads rolling down a hill.

The Shepherd's Homeland

I say:

You play the panpipe for the sheep.
You feed them hot oatmeal.
You weave them wool caps with red and blue tassels.
You whisper and laugh with them.
Why do you pamper them so?

The shepherd says:

In Peru, my homeland
high in the Andes, our sheep thrive.
We treat them with care:
hot food, wool caps, conversation, serenades.
The owners here in Nevada do not believe in song.

I say:

I know Anglo owners.
They care only about profits, nothing else.
Happy sheep? Sad sheep? They don't give a damn.
They hate your excesses, how you indulge the sheep.
They say you've lived among them far too long.

The shepherd says:

I do live with my sheep, know
their names, their sorrows, their joy.
They are creatures, like us.
I whisper my secrets to them
and they whisper theirs to me.

The Prince of Osaka

At the end of my journey, there is a greeting.

In the waiting room of Kansai International Airport
four research assistants stand before me.
Smiles, bows, hellos, thank yous.
Your host had an urgent meeting,
so sorry, he sent us instead.
I'm inspected, almost dissected.
At dinner the menu offers *namako*,
a local specialty. One of the assistants
consults the Japanese-English lexicon
in his hand-held microcomputer and says,
Please taste this delicacy you call slug.
More crunchy than expected,
the slug receives my praise.
Next day, another assistant finds
a tastier translation, sea cucumber.

At the director's office
of the National Museum of Ethnology (MINPAKU)
there is a ceremonial exchange of calling cards.
Smiles, bows, hellos, thank yous, and green tea.
With associates and students present
the director and I speak high solemnity.
Students serve another cup of green tea,
associates leave, formality diminishes,
the director and I joke and laugh.
All present enter the museum, flash photo,
the director leaves, urgent business.
The students say, *Next time buy a ticket, skip*
the director's office, enjoy the exhibits.

I ask the research assistants to show me Osaka profundo.
Smiles, bows, hellos, thank yous, and laughter.
At a photo exhibit of ancient temples,
an assistant says, *Notice how in each photo*
light and blossoms reveal season and time of day.
And a nearby supermarket, like a haiku,
displays asparagus and coho salmon to mark the season.
At a public bath I loll in a pool of hot water.
In a warm foot bath I inhale aromas
of peppermint, thyme, and myrtle.
I laugh when pampered, witnesses chuckle
at my pleasure being naked in public.

Red Bay Summer

I arrive. The cottage shivers. It's been locked since fall.
My broom gathers dark mounds, flies under windows,
spiders bundled in their legs. The lake is gray, grass high.

On the lawn, a fat crow swaggers.
On haunches, the brown rabbit nibbles a dandelion stem,
working from base to fluffy white ball at the top.

On my bike, I reach Oliphant where kiteboarders vault.
Gusts buckle my leg. I smack the pavement, strewn.
My fingers ooze blood, the bicycle shaking on its side.
The bike is new, undented, reliable gears, wide seat,
not enough to make up for my bad right leg.

A man stops his car.
That tumble let you know you're alive, eh?
He chuckles, touches my palm, a minimalist benediction.
His name is Charlie. He demands I see his man cave handiwork.

He wintered in this basement and built a rowboat,
     thin strips of wood
carved just so, bent and aligned with vice grips,
nine coats of shellac, each coat finely sanded,
precision and persistence his twin rules.

The first day of spring he rowed his new boat
and has done so every morning since, faster than a canoe.
He catches bass where his neighbors and I find not a nibble.
His side pockets bulge with tools. His shoes are made
for outdoor work, not for style or dance. He'd prefer
not to be noticed, never be the center of attention.

Possessed by a mood of sincere advice-giving,
Charlie lounges his arm on my shoulders, tells
me I must winter in Red Bay, assist (he means
sand and shellac) in making his next rowboat.
He'll work from fine detailed pencil drawings
by a nineteenth-century draftsman, none better.
His coaching goes on. I must learn the names of the
flora and fauna in his habitat. My wife, Mary, is from here
and willing to teach names. We go on the water.

Grass clings to my paddle as I leave Sucker Creek.
In the bush a red-winged blackbird.
Marsh marigold, lily of the valley, columbine.

I circle Hodgins Lake, avoid beaver lodge,
reeds, leafless trees, their roots under water.
Forget-me-not, false Solomon's seal.

A loon hoots nearby, I can see him.
The kayak glides smooth and silent over gray pond.
Indian paintbrush, Jack-in-the-pulpit.

Slow flap of blue heron flying low,
a great turtle descends the big rock,
horizon clouds, raindrops spatter.

After the Storm

After the storm
expect moisture and serenity,
a tantrum followed by an embrace.
Nature oscillates between
turbulence and calm.
Perhaps the storm is a cleansing
after the accumulation of debris.
Now the Gila monster flicks its tongue.
Now a whiptail lizard swivels its head.
Now sandhill cranes dance in the pasture.

Over the Bridge

Beneath the Brooklyn Bridge at night
a pink flamingo strides across a rock,

spindle legs bent back, artful
neck a rounded echo of its legs, beak

curves down, shading white, brown, black.
The flamingo attracts ogling pedestrians

on their way from Manhattan, wondering
where the bird came from, what it's

doing here, what it has to tell.
The mayor, what's-his-name, asks

why this fuchsia intrusion, what has
dragged it into the metropolis if not

the magnetic pull of the city and why
are its eyes beady and on both sides

of its head and why does it have
three toes and why on this night of all

foggy nights is it so hard to discern
through the haze of headlights,

barely visible as people walk
the bridge to wait for pizza at Grimaldi's.

III

Judith Bishop

I rewrite, but can't tell if I'm making
my poems better or worse. I need help.

The free local paper lists a reading
at the nearby Lutheran church.

I ask one of the readers
if he's in a group. He says, *Yes.*
I decide to be there, silent.

I ask friends to recommend a poetry teacher.
They suggest Judith and I call her.

She says, *Read at Waverly, then
I'll decide whether or not to take you on.*

Judith and I meet once a month.
She writes over my poems in black ink.

She tells me, *Use no more words
than you absolutely need.*

Ode to the Short Line in the Short Poem

You get to the point,
presence and clarity your virtues,
you are accessible,
your usual term of praise,
oscillates
in meaning
between trite and substantial.

Short line,
you wait,
impatient to be written,
your words so few,
each one precious, as Judith taught,
you waste not a syllable,
no syllable wasted.

Your distant cousin,
the long line in the long poem,
rarely arrives,
dresses in her meander of parenthetical asides,
located on a Parisian boulevard,
or a Bogart film noir.

She changes the subject,
waxes wacky, sexy, or surreal.
She is the Gothic cathedral
to your Romanesque abode,
the baroque façade
to your adobe home.

Looking for Lorca

I.

In Granada, Federico García Lorca,
name of airport, the cultural center, park,
a museum, once his family's summer home.
Inside: a wooden desk, his theater company's poster,
his drawings, photographs, his piano.
Fitting tribute, the city's favorite son.
But remember August 1936,
his murder in nearby hills next to an olive tree,
Franco's Falange determined
to make Spain great again.

II.

Twice they look for him at home,
find he's with friends, lock him up,
then one obscure night fascist assault guards pound
on the jailhouse door, *en la puerta golpeaban,*
pirate the poet in an automobile,
force a confession:
socialist, Freemason, homosexual.
Headlights glare,
Lorca still in pajamas,
military orders, instant firing squad
formed by locals—civilians and police.
When challenged, the Generalísimo declares,
"These are natural accidents of war."

III.

Seven years before the fact, Lorca writes
prophetic verses, "I realized I'd been murdered,
but they never found me."

IV.

Atrocity breeds opacity.
Archeologists, forensic anthropologists, historians,
eyewitnesses, journalists, bulldozers search
for remains, come up with only maddening murk.
Local legend, pride laced with shame, stitched
for eighty years, whispers
what nobody knows, says, one night,
a month after his execution, Lorca's family lifts
body from shallow grave, buries
it under their parlor, humming his deep song.

Patricia Spears Jones, Sandra Cisneros, Yusef Komunyakaa, Naomi Shihab Nye, and Mary Louise Pratt have given comments that have enlivened this manuscript. Thank you. I am grateful.

Audiobook

Use the above QR code to access the author reading *Into the World Outspread* in its entirety.

About the author

Renato Rosaldo is Emeritus Professor of Anthropology at New York University and the author of five books of poetry, including *The Chasers*, *The Day of Shelly's Death*, and this one. His bilingual book, *Prayer to Spider Woman/Rezo a la mujer araña*, won the American Book Award in 2004. *Diego Luna's Insider Tips* won the Many Mountains Moving Poetry Book Manuscript Prize, selected by Martin Espada.

Casa Urraca Press

Casa Urraca Press publishes creative nonfiction, poetry, photography, and other works by authors we believe in. New Mexico and the U.S. Southwest are rich in creative and literary talent, and the rest of the world deserves to experience our perspectives. So we champion books that belong in the conversation—books with the power, compassion, and variety to bring very different people closer together.

We are proudly centered in the high desert somewhere near Abiquiú, New Mexico. Find us on social media @casaurracaltd and online at casaurracapress.com for exquisite editions of our books and to register for workshops with our authors.